After the Surge

The Case for U.S. Military Disengagement from Iraq

Steven N. Simon

CSR NO. 23, FEBRUARY 2007 *with new Foreword by the author, September 2007*
COUNCIL ON FOREIGN RELATIONS

Founded in 1921, the Council on Foreign Relations is an independent, national membership organization and a nonpartisan center for scholars dedicated to producing and disseminating ideas so that individual and corporate members, as well as policymakers, journalists, students, and interested citizens in the United States and other countries, can better understand the world and the foreign policy choices facing the United States and other governments. The Council does this by convening meetings; conducting a wide-ranging Studies program; publishing *Foreign Affairs*, the preeminent journal covering international affairs and U.S. foreign policy; maintaining a diverse membership; sponsoring Independent Task Forces and Special Reports; and providing up-to-date information about the world and U.S. foreign policy on the Council's website, www.cfr.org.

THE COUNCIL TAKES NO INSTITUTIONAL POSITION ON POLICY ISSUES AND HAS NO AFFILIATION WITH THE U.S. GOVERNMENT. ALL STATEMENTS OF FACT AND EXPRESSIONS OF OPINION CONTAINED IN ITS PUBLICATIONS ARE THE SOLE RESPONSIBILITY OF THE AUTHOR OR AUTHORS.

Council Special Reports (CSRs) are concise policy briefs, produced to provide a rapid response to a developing crisis or contribute to the public's understanding of current policy dilemmas. CSRs are written by individual authors—who may be Council fellows or acknowledged experts from outside the institution—in consultation with an advisory committee, and typically take sixty days or less from inception to publication. The committee serves as a sounding board and provides feedback on a draft report. It usually meets twice—once before a draft is written and once again when there is a draft for review; however, advisory committee members, unlike Task Force members, are not asked to sign off on the report or to otherwise endorse it. Once published, CSRs are posted on the Council's website.

For further information about the Council or this Special Report, please write to the Council on Foreign Relations, 58 East 68th Street, New York, NY 10021, or call the Communications office at 212-434-9400. Visit our website at CFR.org.

CONTENTS

New Foreword by the Author   v

Foreword   ix

Acknowledgments   xi

Maps   xii

List of Acronyms   xv

Council Special Report   1

    After the Surge   3

    The Problems Faced by the United States in Iraq   12

    The Case for Disengagement   24

    Recommendations   39

Advisory Committee Members   45

About the Author   47

NEW FOREWORD BY THE AUTHOR

Steven N. Simon

September 2007

When this Council Special Report (CSR) was first issued in February 2007, the debate over the surge was raging. President George W. Bush had only announced his intention to deploy additional troops. Democrats and Republicans rushed to the barricades either to deplore or to defend it. This report, however, saw the surge as inevitable—since its opponents were powerless to stop it—and, more importantly, as beside the point. Hence its title, *After the Surge*.

The core issue then, as now, was whether the government in Baghdad would pursue a compelling program of national reconciliation. In February, this report argued that necessary conditions for reconciliation were unlikely to emerge for some time. The importance of this point was dictated by the administration's justification for the surge: to provide the government in Baghdad the political space in which to advance its reconciliation agenda. Space, in this case, would take the form of a downturn in the level of violence, which was presumed to be a serious impediment to compromise across sectarian lines. The CSR's focus on what would happen after the surge reflected an assumption that even after several months, surge results would be inconclusive at best.

From the perspective of the report, there was never any question that areas flooded with well-led, heavily armed U.S. troops using appropriate tactics would see less sectarian violence. Predictably, the levels of bloodshed in localities to which troops were surged are presently below the spike of December 2006. Violence is now back to what it was in the summer of 2006, when it was still regarded as unacceptably high.[1] In any case, it is the absolute level of violence that matters and the absolute level is still incompatible

---

[1] How much lower is unclear, especially since Central Command (CENTCOM) does not count intra-sectarian violence, which by all accounts has mushroomed in 2007. CENTCOM's estimate employs counting rules that appear to exclude deaths resulting from criminal action, despite the uncertain dividing line between criminal and political murders. In some areas, killing and displacement have diminished because, as ethnic cleansing succeeds, there are diminishing numbers of prospective victims for attackers to target. See Karen DeYoung, "Experts Doubt Drop in Violence in Iraq," *Washington Post*, September 6, 2007, p. A16; and General Accountability Office (GAO) report, *Securing, Stabilizing, and Rebuilding Iraq: Iraqi Government Has Not Met Most Legislative, Security, and Economic Benchmarks*, GAO-07-1230T, September 7, 2007.

with security and political stability in Iraq. To be successful, the surge would have to lessen violence to the point at which a functioning state might be able to emerge. Given that there are no more U.S. forces available for this mission, this outcome must be considered remote.

Even if the surge were to reduce violence significantly, or pacify territory, two additional requirements would still have to be met for victory to be within reach. First, Iraqi forces would have to be capable of consolidating these gains. Second, an Iraqi government, alive to the opportunities created by the surge, would have to move quickly to implement reforms. As the Report of the Independent Commission on the Security Forces of Iraq states unambiguously, Iraqi forces are unprepared to preserve U.S. gains in the security arena. And as the GAO report, as well as the new National Intelligence Estimate and the administration's own complaints about Prime Minister Nuri al-Maliki, makes clear, the Iraqi government has failed to seize the day.

This should come as no surprise. The full reports of General David H. Petraeus and U.S. Ambassador to Iraq Ryan C. Crocker spotlight the chasm that separates U.S. and Iraqi conceptions of reconciliation. For Americans, reconciliation is the product of a bargaining process through which Sunnis participate in the governance of the state and get their fair share of Iraq's resources.

Iraqis continue to see things differently. Shias have tended to emphasize the need for justice. The centrality of justice is rooted in the history of Shia thought and in their painful experience as Iraqis. For them, justice demands that their suffering under previous regimes be compensated. This in turn necessitates the subordination of Iraq's Sunni population to the needs of the Shia community. For the Shia-run government, justice must precede reconciliation.

For many Sunnis, reconciliation means restoration. This goes beyond mere inclusion in power-sharing arrangements. It means regaining control of the state. Cutting al-Qaeda down to size and placating U.S. commanders are a means to that end. For Kurds, reconciliation means recognition of Kurdish autonomy and openness to the Kurds' prospective territorial (and concomitant economic) gains.

These differences will not be reconciled anytime soon. Dethroned elites do not easily surrender their dreams of a reversal of fortune. The agonizing process that now grips

Iraqi Sunnis resembles the way people are said to grapple with imminent death—through stages of denial, anger, bargaining, depression, and acceptance. Sunnis are not yet near the bargaining stage of internalizing the fact of Saddam's overthrow.

The only new development since this report was issued has been Washington's attempt to balance its interests in Iraq by courting Sunni tribes. Who, after all, could misinterpret the symbolism of President Bush landing in Anbar province before proceeding to Shia Baghdad? Yet this move has made Sunni acceptance of the new order even more remote, even as it has amplified Shia distrust and intransigence. The empowerment of Sunni tribes as a tactical weapon against al-Qaeda has produced gains on the ground, but will likely sabotage the longer-term U.S. strategic objective of a unitary Iraq. Indeed, by supporting Sunnis, the United States inadvertently vindicates hardliners in that community who think they might get their way, thereby undermining the eventual emergence of a stable polity.

Thus, Americans are left with the same questions they faced at the start of the year:

- If the Iraqi political center cannot hold, then what purpose do U.S. military forces serve in Iraq?
- If these forces cannot reconstitute a unitary Iraqi state, what sort of pathway to withdrawal will be least costly to the United States and Iraq?
- In the interim between a decision to withdraw and the departure of the last GI, what should U.S. diplomatic and military priorities be?

The recommendations put forward by this report eight months ago still stand. The U.S. presence in Iraq is hostage to fortune. To withdraw in an orderly fashion, on a U.S. timetable, remains the best way to avoid being forced out, either by events on the ground in Iraq, or by a seismic shift in public opinion at home, or both. A panicked rush to the exits could carry a high price in blood and reputation. Moreover, the United States will still have an abiding interest in Iraq, even if it cannot secure its interest militarily. The withdrawal process, therefore, will have to proceed in tandem with an interlinked diplomatic, economic, and counterterrorism program that reduces U.S. liabilities and preserves its interests within Iraq and the wider region in the years ahead.

As earlier in 2007, the calculation policymakers must make is whether the demonstrated costs of staying are greater than the postulated costs of a careful drawdown. As before, the best way to minimize these postulated risks is still to prepare carefully and act deliberately. Washington must put more thought into how it gets out of Iraq than it put into getting into Iraq. This cannot be done by perpetually postponing the day of reckoning. Despite marginal gains, the surge has only postponed an inevitable U.S. drawdown. With the collapse of public support for the war and confidence in the president, the question is not whether the U.S. military will be removed from Iraq, but only when and under what circumstances. The sooner America's decision-makers come to grips with this reality, the better.

FOREWORD

Iraq has come to dominate U.S. foreign policy—and the controversy over Iraq has come to dominate the debate over U.S. foreign policy. This report by Steven N. Simon, the Hasib J. Sabbagh Senior Fellow for Middle Eastern Studies at the Council on Foreign Relations, makes a major contribution to that debate.

After the Surge: The Case for U.S. Military Disengagement from Iraq is premised on the judgment that the United States is not succeeding in Iraq and that Iraq itself is more divided and violent than ever. It concludes that the administration's decision to increase U.S. force levels will fail to prevent further deterioration in the situation—and that there is no alternative policy with the potential to turn things around.

As a result, Simon urges the United States to disengage militarily from Iraq, a disengagement that in his view should involve a negotiated accord with Iraq's government, a dialogue with Iraq's neighbors, and new diplomatic initiatives throughout the region. Simon argues that if the United States does all this, it can minimize the strategic costs of its failure in Iraq and even offset these losses in whole or in part.

I expect that many readers will disagree with some of Simon's analysis or his proposals. But I am confident that every reader will benefit from his deep and broad knowledge, his penetrating analysis, and the challenge of his arguments. This is an important paper written in a compelling manner about a critical issue.

Richard N. Haass
President
Council on Foreign Relations
February 2007

ACKNOWLEDGMENTS

This report benefited greatly from the expertise of others. Toby Dodge of the International Institute for Strategic Studies and Queen Mary's College, University of London contributed his analysis of the sources of Iraq's political troubles. His deep knowledge of Iraqi history and close reading of post-intervention developments in that sad country were invaluable. The Advisory Committee was uniformly generous with its time and candid counsel. I would particularly like to thank Dana Allin, Daniel Benjamin, F. Gregory Gause III, Philip H. Gordon, Mohammed Hafez, Joost Hiltermann, Ellen Laipson, Mark Lynch, Steven E. Miller, Barry R. Posen, James Spencer, and Jonathan Stephenson for their wise guidance. My Council colleagues—Richard N. Haass, Stephen Biddle, Lee Feinstein, Sara B. Moller, William L. Nash, Vali R. Nasr, Divya Reddy, Gary Samore, and Ray Takeyh—won my gratitude for their strong support and sound advice. Thanks also to Anya Schmemann of the Communications department, who has worked to ensure that this report is read outside the remote fastnesses of the Council, and to Patricia Dorff and Lia Norton in the Publications department, who provided crucial assistance in the production of this document. Although the strengths of this report are attributable to others, its weaknesses are entirely mine.

Steven N. Simon

MAPS

Source: UN Department of Peacekeeping Cartographic Section, Map No. 3835 (January 2004), www.un.org/depts/cartographic/map/profile/iraq.pdf.

Map 1: Iraq

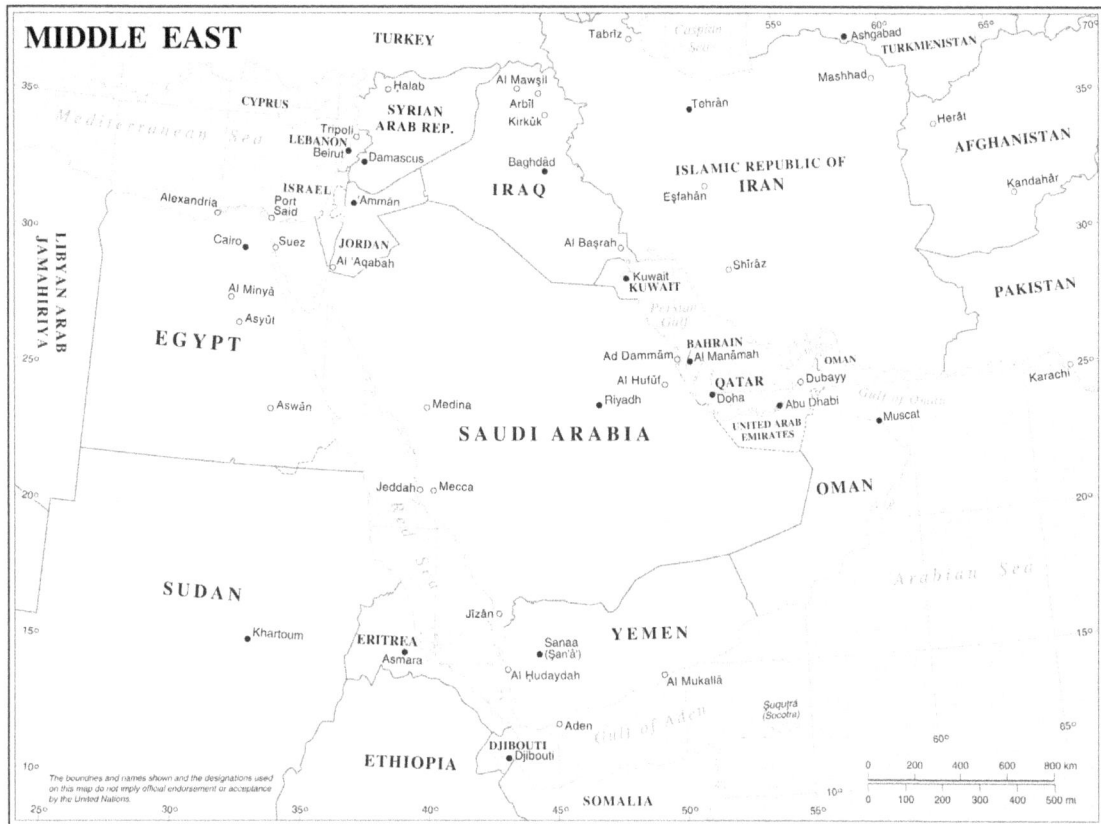

Source: UN Department of Peacekeeping Cartographic Section, Map No. 4102 (August 2004), www.un.org/Depts/Cartographic/map/profile/mideastr.pdf.

Map 2: Regional Perspective

LIST OF ACRONYMS

BIAP	Baghdad International Airport
CPA	Coalition Provisional Authority
EU	European Union
GCC	Gulf Cooperation Council
GDP	gross domestic product
GIA	Armed Islamic Group
IED	improvised explosive device
KDP	Kurdish Democratic Party
NGO	nongovernmental organization
NIE	National Intelligence Estimate
PRT	provincial reconstruction team
PUK	Patriotic Union of Kurdistan
SCIRI	Supreme Council for the Islamic Revolution in Iraq
UIA	United Iraqi Alliance
UNAMI	United Nations Assistance Mission in Iraq
USAID	United States Agency for International Development

COUNCIL SPECIAL REPORT

AFTER THE SURGE

The American intervention in Iraq unseated a murderous despot in April 2003. It also triggered the collapse of the Iraqi state, plunged the country into a civil war that brought about the deaths of tens of thousands of Iraqi civilians, wrecked the country's already debilitated infrastructure, and spurred violent sectarian rivalries that threatened to spill over into the broader Middle East.

The crisis has now moved beyond the capacity of Washington to control on its own. The results of the midterm elections show that public support for the present course has buckled. The United States lacks the military resources and the domestic and international political support to master the situation. The number of U.S. troops presently in Iraq, 134,000, allows commanders on the ground little room to maneuver. The disappointing results of Operation Together Forward in Baghdad showed that while U.S. forces can concentrate for a limited amount of time in a small number of targeted sectors, they lack the numbers to stabilize even those areas on a lasting basis. The 21,500 additional soldiers proposed by the Bush administration to fill the "five brigade" gap in Baghdad fall far short of the total needed to tip the long-term balance toward peace within Baghdad, let alone the country as a whole. Assuming it were possible to restore order in Iraq, the task, according to the army's new counterinsurgency manual drafted under then Lieutenant General David H. Petraeus's supervision, would require at least double the number of troops the United States will have on the ground once the latest surge has been implemented. A commitment this big would force the United States to reduce its forward deployed forces in other areas where they safeguard American interests.

The U.S. Army and Marine Corps are too compact to meet the labor-intensive challenge of state building in Iraq. This is true as well for the State Department's civilian resources. To foster reconstruction of a country with 28.8 million people, the United States has authorized 167 non-Defense Department civilians, alongside 178 soldiers, to work in provincial reconstruction teams (PRTs). It has managed to fill 116 of these civilian positions. For a perspective on this commitment, consider Vietnam in 1969—then a country of 18 million—when the State Department had 1,700 personnel alongside 6,400 troops in Civil Operations and Revolutionary Development Support teams, the equivalent of today's PRTs. President George W. Bush's declared intention to double the small number of PRTs in Iraq shows an awareness of the importance of reconstruction, but underestimates the difficulty the State Department has faced in recruiting qualified officers for service in Iraq. In the late 1960s, one of every twenty-five State Department or United States Agency for International Development (USAID) employees was in Vietnam; in Iraq's PRTs, the ratio is 1 to 333. The level of reconstruction assistance tells the same story. The president's pledge of more than $1 billion in additional funds represents a mere rounding error compared to previous allocations, and seems unrelated to the magnitude of current needs. Again, for comparison, the United States spent 2 percent of gross domestic product (GDP) on economic and military assistance to Vietnam, but less than one-fifth of 1 percent for Iraq. If the consequences of defeat in Iraq are in fact "incalculable," as Secretary of Defense Robert M. Gates has told Congress, the gap between the presumed strategic stakes and the U.S. level of effort is striking. Lamentably, the erosion of public support for the war and confidence in the president's judgment have probably ruled out the possibility of bridging the chasm between resources and requirements.

Arguably, this mismatch might prove to be irrelevant, given that the challenge of counterinsurgency where there is no indigenous government to support on the battlefield and the rigors of combat must be borne by the outsider alone is too steep for democracies, especially in a world of globalized media. The United States does not have the same room to maneuver that Britain enjoyed in its counterinsurgency operations in Kenya or Malaya. The American public will eventually fault battlefield excesses or abuses inflicted in cellars—the ineluctable by-products of such wars—if the strategic goal is seen to be inessential. It will not long tolerate casualties if it sees its leaders openly divided about the stakes and they have lost faith in the possibility of victory. Bipartisan nonbinding congressional resolutions opposing the surge of U.S. troops to Baghdad will further erode lingering public confidence in the American venture in Iraq.

Even if the United States had the abundant ground forces and reconstruction teams necessary, it is not clear that the situation in Iraq today is retrievable. Twenty-three years of Saddam's rule had already dismantled civil society before twelve years of sanctions hollowed out Iraq's middle class. U.S. intervention decapitated its leadership, swept aside its remaining institutions, and created the security vacuum that empowered militias and reduced society to a state of Hobbesian misery.

Iraqis have thus been stripped of the capacity to build a post-Ba'athist state. At this point, a political settlement would have to involve agreement within and then among three of four major warring constituencies in Iraq. These groups do not have the internal cohesion, let alone the interest in a nationwide consensus, to negotiate a sustainable deal. The Kurdish leadership and the senior echelons of the main Shia party, the Supreme Council for the Islamic Revolution in Iraq (SCIRI), agree on autonomy and control of their respective oil fields. The urbanized Arab Shia in Baghdad, who Muqtada al-Sadr claims to represent, seek a centralized state empowered by oil revenues, as do the Arab Sunnis. But they disagree on who should run it. Both factions oppose the separatist impulse among the Kurds and segments of the Shia population based in Basra. Secular nationalists, symbolized by Iyad Allawi, who sought to mobilize what was left of the middle class, failed and, along with the majority of Iraq's Christians, have fled the country. In a society beset by state collapse and rising sectarian violence, there is no plausible coalition that would be sufficiently inclusive.

As these political fissures have widened, ministries of the nascent state have become more deeply implicated in the savage violence sweeping through Baghdad. The government is paralyzed. Iraqi Prime Minister Nouri Kamel al-Maliki cannot move against the militias or adopt a conciliatory posture toward Sunnis without alienating his base of support. The militias themselves are splintering along lines of turf and ideology and are less responsive to the political guidance of their leaders within the government. U.S. forces, too, are paralyzed. They have been reduced to bystanders amid rampant abductions, pogroms, mass executions, and ethnic cleansing. The inability of U.S. forces to provide basic human security surely has contributed to the anti-American sentiment revealed in successive polls: A majority of respondents say that killing Americans in Iraq is justifiable.

THE CASE FOR DISENGAGEMENT

The United States has already achieved all that it is likely to achieve in Iraq: the removal of Saddam, the end of the Ba'athist regime, the elimination of the Iraqi regional threat, the snuffing out of Iraq's unrequited aspiration to weapons of mass destruction, and the opening of a door, however narrow, to a constitutionally based electoral democracy. Staying in Iraq can only drive up the price of these gains in blood, treasure, and strategic position. Any realistic reckoning for the future will have to acknowledge six grim realities:

- The United States cannot determine political outcomes or achieve its remaining political aims via military means. American military forces have not brought the violence to an end or under control and will not do so in the future. In the absence of the understanding and the intelligence needed to operate effectively in the complex and violent political situation in Iraq, this should not be surprising.

- Leaving U.S. forces in Iraq under today's circumstances means the United States is culpable but not capable—that is, Washington bears substantial responsibility for developments within Iraq without the ability to shape those developments in a positive direction. In consequence, Iraqi support for the U.S. presence has collapsed. Polls indicate that most Iraqis want the United States to pull out. Moreover, the Iraq war has fueled the jihad and apparently been a godsend to jihadi recruiters—and the process of self-recruitment—as indicated by the 2006 National Intelligence Estimate (NIE) on the global war on terror. More broadly, the Iraq war has had a very damaging effect on the U.S. reputation in the Arab and wider Islamic world. Authoritative opinion surveys show this as well. The continued presence of U.S. forces is thus a severe setback in the canonical war of ideas, which the Bush administration has correctly assessed as crucial to American interests.

- The ongoing war has empowered and advanced the interests of the chief U.S. rival in the region, Iran. At this stage, the best way to regulate Iran's attempts to exploit its advantages is to negotiate with Tehran either bilaterally or in a multilateral framework while protecting Americans in Iraq against Iranian attack.

- By siphoning resources and political attention away from Afghanistan, a continuing military commitment to Iraq may lead to two U.S. losses in southwest Asia.

- The Iraq war constrains the U.S. military, making it very difficult if not impossible to handle another significant contingency involving ground forces. It also damages the U.S. military, making it difficult for Washington to credibly employ coercive policies against others in the near to medium term even once the United States has disengaged from Iraq. Furthermore, the military commitment in Iraq impedes the U.S. ability to address other important international contingencies, in part because of the limitations of the U.S. military but also because of the preoccupation with Iraq at the highest decision-making levels. In short, U.S. interests in the Middle East and Persian Gulf region can be more effectively advanced if the United States disengages from Iraq. Indeed, the sooner Washington grasps this nettle, the sooner it can begin to repair the damage that has been done to America's international position. Staying longer means more damage and a later start on repair.

- The implosion of domestic support for the war will compel the disengagement of U.S. forces; it is now just a matter of time. Better to withdraw as a coherent and at least somewhat volitional act than withdraw later in hectic response to public opposition to the war in the United States or to a series of unexpectedly sharp reverses on the ground in Iraq.

The United States should therefore make clear now to the Iraqi government that, as the results of the anticipated surge become apparent, the two sides will begin to negotiate a U.S. military disengagement from Iraq. That would entail withdrawing the bulk of American forces from Iraq within twelve to eighteen months (that is to say, over the course of calendar year 2008); shifting the American focus to containment of the conflict and strengthening the U.S. military position elsewhere in the region; and engaging Iraq's neighbors, including Iran and Syria, members of the UN Security Council, and potential donors in an Iraq stabilization plan.

Since the surge is a fait accompli, according to the vice president, and its results will be known very soon, in the view of General Petraeus, there is little point in proposing that negotiation of a drawdown begin immediately. The prospect of disengagement, however, should be a matter of discussion with the Iraqi government now. (If Secretary Gates's January 12, 2006, Senate testimony is accurate, then the drawdown of U.S. forces might begin within one year, although nothing is known about the administration's longer-range planning estimates apart from Secretary Gates's denial that the United States sought permanent bases in Iraq.)

The proposed military disengagement would not be linked to benchmarks that the Iraqi government is probably incapable of fulfilling. This analysis differs from the Bush administration's new strategy in its repudiation of the idea that victory in Iraq, however defined, can be won militarily. More specifically, it departs from current policy in terms of the unconditional nature of the proposed disengagement, skepticism about the relevance of benchmarks, severe doubts about the utility of a temporary buildup, and strong reservations about the feasibility of further large-scale training efforts. Both the "Go Long" option—named after a football play that aims for a sizable gain from a single pass—which would combine a slight increase in U.S. forces in the short term with a longer-term intensive commitment to training Iraqi troops and "Double Down"—referring to a gambling term that signifies doubling a bet on the basis of a promising but incomplete blackjack hand—are unworkable. Proponents of these tactical departures assert that the security situation, particularly in Baghdad, impedes political compromise. This analysis, in contrast, acknowledges the reciprocal relationship between security and political progress, but sees the security situation since early 2006 more as the effect of an Iraqi political process that failed to unify the country during the previous two years than the cause of the Maliki government's current weakness.

It would be irresponsible to dismiss the grave scenario depicted by the administration and many other observers as the most likely consequence of a rapid U.S. military drawdown: dramatically greater levels of violence, an emboldened al-Qaeda with a new base from which to operate, an isolated Kurdish north, the intervention of neighboring countries, and regional chaos. The new National Intelligence Estimate on Iraq asserts that a rapid withdrawal of U.S. troops could set in motion more intensive violence and ethnic cleansing, "political disarray," and possibly Turkish intervention. For these reasons, the NIE concludes that the presence of coalition military forces continues to be "an essential stabilizing element." Yet, as the NIE stresses, there was a "sea change" in the level of violence last year amid a large number of active coalition troops. The Iraqi Security Forces, which the NIE judges to be infected with debilitating sectarian loyalties and of little reliability, are put forward as a potential casualty of a U.S. drawdown, despite their currently parlous state and the intelligence community's estimate that these forces would not be able to function effectively as a national, nonsectarian force for years to come.

A truly rapid withdrawal is not endorsed in this report. But raising the prospect of desperate deterioration in Iraq and its environs after an American military disengagement necessarily tends to obscure two things. First, the presence of U.S. forces has not stabilized Iraq thus far. Second, conditions for instability have become structural elements of Iraqi politics.

Given these facts, how long should the U.S. keep troops in Iraq, when its military presence only delays an inevitable escalation of intra-Iraqi fighting?

Military disengagement will be a severe blow to the United States, which staked its prestige and defined its security on the basis of a war to disarm Iraq and transform its politics. Disengaging will signify the inability to achieve these strategic goals. American resolve will likely be questioned. In the near to medium term, this could make it harder, perhaps much harder, to influence Middle Eastern governments when Washington most needs their cooperation to stabilize Iraq and push back against Iran, without further stoking regional sectarian rivalries. The dismal irony is this: Proponents of an indefinite commitment of U.S. forces seek above all to preserve the core American interest in demonstrating resolve; but that demonstration cannot ultimately be sustained and, in any case, has been devalued by the fundamentally flawed nature of the intervention and its aftermath. The jihadis already believe that they have won while Iran is convinced that it has the upper hand, despite the tenacity of U.S. troops on the ground in Iraq.

It is possible that neighboring countries will intensify their competition by proxy within Iraq and foster even greater violence. The problem to fear is the transfer of heavy weapons to the contending factions by outside supporters. The more heavily armed the combatants are, the more noncombatant casualties will result from the fighting. U.S. and UK forces, however, have not been notably successful in controlling the borders thus far. This is a hazard that will have to be contained primarily through regional diplomacy backed by accurate intelligence.

The Turks are apprehensive about the transformation of Iraq and might be tempted to intervene if they perceive a Kurdish state with significant resources rising from the wreckage of a sinking Iraqi state. This would not be in the U.S. interest, but many Turks know that an intervention would be no less a disaster for them than it was for the United States. A reflexive Turkish invasion of northern Iraq is not an ineluctable result of American disengagement.

Jordan, an important U.S. ally, has been imperiled by the war, in part because it has been the object of attacks by the Zarqawi network and, perhaps more dangerously, has emerged as the obvious destination for an estimated 750,000 refugees, over 10 percent of its indigenous population. U.S. forces, in their current numbers and configuration, are not going to solve this problem. Until Iraqi politics cohere, Jordan most needs financial aid and competent technical assistance to house, sustain, and control the second and third waves of refugees who lack resources of their own. The fact is that long-term prospects for the Sunni states friendly to the

United States may be clouded, but they are unlikely to face unmanageable subversive challenges as a consequence of an orderly U.S. disengagement from Iraq over a twelve-to-eighteen-month period.

Although a regional conflagration is conceivable, it is not the likeliest consequence of civil war in the Middle East. Civil wars in the Middle East have not been rare occurrences, yet with the partial exception of the Lebanese civil war, which involved Israel and Syria, such wars have largely been contained within the divided state itself. Nor have wars between states submerged the entire region in violent disorder. The Iran-Iraq war raged for a decade but did not engulf the region. Arab-Israeli wars have not led to inter-Arab wars. Indeed, the only recent aggressor in this mode was Saddam Hussein, when he attacked Kuwait in 1990. Arguably, that war did engender a broader conflict—in the form of a sustained al-Qaeda campaign against the United States—but it did not turn into a regional war.

In 2004, Ayman al-Zawahiri, the deputy to Osama bin Laden, said of the U.S. intervention: "America is between two fires. If it stays in Iraq, it will bleed to death; if it leaves, it will lose everything." His forecast comes disturbingly close to describing current circumstances. It need not, however, be prophecy. More than three years after the intervention began, to be sure, the United States finds itself in an agonizing strategic position. The time has come to acknowledge that the United States must fundamentally recast its commitment to Iraq. It must do so without any illusions that there are unexplored or magic fixes, whether diplomatic or military. Some disasters are irretrievable. Having staked its prestige on the intervention and failed to achieve many of its objectives, the United States will certainly pay a price for military disengagement from Iraq. But if the United States manages its departure from Iraq carefully, it will not have lost everything. Rather, the United States will have preserved the opportunity to recover vital assets that its campaign in Iraq has imperiled: diplomatic initiative, global reputation, and the well-being and political utility of its ground forces.

THE PROBLEMS FACED BY THE UNITED STATES IN IRAQ

The United States finds itself in a dire position in Iraq today because of two interlinked problems that it has been unable to solve. The roots of both problems lie not in the malign intervention of either Iran or Syria, although these states have undoubtedly exploited the demise of the Ba'athist regime, but within Iraq itself. The first of these problems is the violence and instability caused by the almost complete collapse of administrative and coercive state capacity in April 2003. The three weeks of looting that erupted in the wake of the liberation of Baghdad shattered the capacity of the state, destroying seventeen out of the twenty-three ministries in the capital, causing an estimated $12 billion in damage. The result is that Iraqi society continues to be dominated by a profound security vacuum. A myriad of armed groups deploying violence for their own gain seized the opportunities provided by the collapse of the state and the disbanding of the Iraqi army.

The second problem, the failure of the politicians now running Iraq to win legitimacy, springs from this lack of governmental capacity. From 1968 until 2003, the Ba'athist government used oil wealth and unprecedented violence to strangle any organizing capacity within Iraqi society. Those who challenged the government were imprisoned, tortured, and murdered or driven into exile. Those who remained in the country came to realize that physical survival and economic well-being depended on their political passivity. As a result of this violence, civil society simply did not exist when the U.S. military reached Baghdad in April 2003. In the aftermath of regime change, Iraqi politics had to start from scratch. The majority of the politicians and parties that now dominate the Iraqi government had been long absent from the country and faced widespread hostility and suspicion on their return.

After three and a half years of U.S. involvement in Iraq, the intertwined problems of weak political legitimacy and intense violence are worsening. The U.S. management of its responsibilities in Iraq since 2003 contributed mightily to this situation. The unwillingness to commit sufficient resources; decision to disband the army and enforce a program of radical de-Ba'athification; entrusting an amateurish American leadership imbued with a grandiose conception of its power and committed to a flawed political program; failure to focus on security and quality of life; and ignorance of the complex realities of Iraqi society helped undermine conditions that might have offset problems of weak Iraqi political legitimacy and ready recourse to violence.

Today, the political parties that claim to represent the population of south and central Iraq have very shallow roots in society. Iraq's Arab politicians, sitting behind the high blast walls that protect the Green Zone, have been unable to form robust links to society as a whole and thereby win acceptance of their authority.

THE PROBLEM WITH IRAQI POLITICS

The intense, yearlong political process of 2005 was meant to confer a degree of legitimacy on a new political elite chosen by the Iraqi people. Although the second set of elections in December 2005, with their high turnout, were a success, the elected government proved to be too divided and corrupt to begin rebuilding the Iraqi state. The five months it took for Iraq's newly elected government to agree on a prime minister was an early sign of trouble.

The long interval between the 2005 elections and the formation of a government in May 2006 was due to the fractious nature of the multiparty coalitions assembled to contest the two elections and disagreement within the victorious Shia coalition, the United Iraqi Alliance (UIA), about who should be prime minister. The Shia leader of the Islamic Dawa Party, Ibrahim al-Jaafari, winner of the previous round of elections in January 2005, had alienated other important politicians, as well as officials in London and Washington. He lacked the personal dynamism and diplomatic skill to weld the disparate political factions that dominate Iraqi politics into a cohesive coalition government. Adel Abdul al-Mahdi, the second-in-command of the Supreme Council for the Islamic Revolution, emerged as a more capable contender for the premiership. Divisions within the UIA meant that neither Jaafari nor Mahdi could gain a decisive majority. Thus, in April 2006, the UIA finally nominated Jaafari's deputy, Nouri al-Maliki, as a compromise candidate. Maliki broke the deadlock and became prime minister because of the support of Muqtada al-Sadr's twenty-eight members of parliament. From that moment, Maliki became dependent on Sadr, his party, and, by implication, Sadr's militia, the Mahdi army.

Maliki, like Jaafari before him, found that the office of prime minister in the new Iraq has little power. In the aftermath of the 2005 elections, real power was divided up among the political parties, with electoral success being rewarded by the spoils of government in the form of cabinet portfolios and the patronage opportunities they provided. Maliki's only leverage over the cabinet, and the government beyond it, stems from his ability to play ministers off against one another or to win limited consensus on the basis of the lowest common denominator—anti-American rhetoric. In the absence of prime ministerial authority or personal scruples, ministers appointed by their parties have a large incentive to strip their ministries. This has further subverted the institutional capacity of the Iraqi state to serve its citizens.

Having acceded to the premiership in late April 2006, Maliki took yet another month to cobble together a government of national unity, carefully rewarding the main parties with sectarian appointments. The weakness of his position was reflected in his inability to discipline or jettison ministers who had proved to be inefficient, dishonest, or controversial during the previous year. The result was a cabinet that placed sectarian maneuvering above the needs of a population traumatized by the collapse of the state in 2003, a crime wave, and the specter of civil war. The role of Bayan Jabor, a prominent member of SCIRI, the largest party in the UIA, and a former senior commander in its militia, the Badr Brigade, illustrates the problem. As minister of Interior in the government of Ibrahim al-Jaafari, Jabor was heavily criticized for sacking many professional staff members and replacing them with his old Badr Brigade comrades. Under his command, the death squads composed of the ministry's special commandos hastened Iraq's descent into civil war. Although Maliki eventually succeeded in moving Jabor from the Interior Ministry, the precarious politics of coalition government meant that Jabor was shifted laterally, to the Ministry of Finance. Maliki's weakness also accounts for his transfer of the ministries of Education and Health to members of Muqtada al-Sadr's organization, which had engaged in two extended and bloody rebellions against the U.S. Army.

Despite two postwar elections, the government in Iraq remains fractious and scandal-ridden. This new governing elite has proved singularly unable to rebuild the state, impose order across the country, or help the vast majority of ordinary immiserated citizens. Iraqis must try to live as best they can without a functioning government, prey to criminals, militias, and insurgents. At the same time, American influence over the government has dwindled. The logic of nationwide elections dictates that Iraqi politicians can circumvent, refuse, or ignore coalition advice.

The Iraqi government's inability to impose law and order on the country has done the most to undermine its popular legitimacy and even its relevance. The looting that began in April 2003 as an exuberant, if lawless, celebration of regime change rapidly degenerated into a crime wave, then an insurgency, and finally civil war. The decision by the Coalition Provisional Authority (CPA) to disband the Iraqi army inflamed the fear and resentment driving insurgent violence. The inability of the U.S. armed forces, and now the Iraqi security services, to impose order on the south and center of the country has given rise to three distinct groups perpetrating violence outside the control of the state: criminal gangs, insurgent groups, and militias.

Saddam Hussein's decision to empty the jails of criminals on the eve of the invasion further complicated a tenuous security situation. The fact that criminal activity is as bad in Basra as in Baghdad indicates both the extent of the problem but also the inability of Iraq's regional police forces to cope with it. What started in 2003 with the looting of government buildings quickly evolved into a crime wave across the whole of south and central Iraq. Armed thugs patrol the streets robbing and killing while gangs of kidnappers run rampant. The prevalence and brutality of these kidnappings has done much to contribute to a general sense of insecurity and driven hundreds of thousands of Iraqis from the country.

Iraqi security forces and the U.S. military have also been unable to tackle the disparate forces that make up the insurgency. Initially reactive and highly localized, the insurgency has grown and spread in recent years as the U.S. military's inability to control Iraq became apparent to the insurgents. At the insurgency's center are a myriad of small fighting groups built around personal ties of trust, cemented by family, locality, or long friendship. At the outset, the insurgency had dozens of autonomous units, with as many as 20,000 to 50,000 fighters in its ranks. Over the past three years, insurgents have learned to deploy innovative technology and tactics to attack U.S. forces and impose relatively high casualties.

From 2005 onward, the insurgents coalesced around a few groups, including the Islamic Army in Iraq, the Partisans of the Sunna army, the Mujahidin's army, Muhammad's army, and Islamic Resistance Movement in Iraq. As their names suggest, the use of violence by the insurgency has been increasingly justified in religious terms. What started as an uprising directed against the U.S. intervention under the banner of Iraqi nationalism has achieved ideological coherence by fusing the powerful appeal of nationalism with an austere Sunni Salafism. The attraction of Salafist doctrine for the insurgents is the strict boundary it draws between those involved in the jihad and those who are not. According to this interpretation of Salafism, those not backing the struggle can be branded as nonbelievers and, as such, executed. The encroachment of Salafism has intensified the inherent bloodthirstiness of the sectarian violence. Shias can be murdered either because they do not follow the "true path of Islam" or because they form the majority of the security forces, or both. The inability of American forces to slow the transformation of the insurgency from liberation movement to sectarian civil war, or to reduce its toxicity, should compound skepticism about their utility in Iraq.

This evolution of the insurgency culminated in the bombing of the al-Askari shrine in the city of Samarra in February 2006. The fierce reaction of Shia groups to the attack showed that a third group using force, the sectarian militias formed by political parties, had begun to rival the insurgents as the dominant sources of violence driving Iraq deeper into civil war. With an estimated 140,000 fighters in their ranks, the militias are overtly organized and legitimized along sectarian lines. In the absence of effective security arrangements, the militias have increased their power and visibility on the streets of Iraq's major towns and cities. Although the sectarian militias enjoy little popular support, their existence testifies powerfully to the inability of the Iraqi government to guarantee the personal safety of its citizens.

Iraq's militias can be divided into three broad groups, depending on their organizational coherence (or lack of it) and relationship to national politics: the Kurdish militias, those affiliated with former exiled parties, and those established in the wake of the intervention. The most centralized forces are the two Kurdish militias of the Kurdistan Democratic Party (KDP) and the Patriotic Union of Kurdistan (PUK). Together their forces number from 80,000 to 100,000 fighters. While the Kurdish militias are the most organized, institutionalized, and comparatively disciplined in the country, the KDP and PUK are staunch rivals. Both groups have a long history of fighting against the central government in Baghdad. They won enclave protection from the United Nations after the 1991 Kurdish uprising. In the 1990s the two parties engaged in a civil war over control of the profits from oil smuggling. The fractured political loyalties at the heart of the Iraqi Kurdish region did not disappear after the fall of the Hussein regime; the two militias remain rivals.

Militias created in exile and brought back to Iraq in the wake of Saddam's fall constitute the second influential group of militias active in Iraq today. The most powerful of these is the Badr Brigade, the military arm of SCIRI, estimated to have at least 10,000 fighters. Like SCIRI, the Badr Brigade was created at the height of the Iranian revolution as a foreign policy tool for the Iranian government. Indeed, the Badr Brigade was trained and officered by the Iranian Revolutionary Guard Corps until many of its fighters began returning to Iraq. The Badr Brigade's integration into the security forces across the south and center of the country, especially the police and paramilitary units associated with the Ministry of Interior, has accelerated the decline of the state-controlled forces of law and order. Several other former exiled parties have also set up militias to provide security for their leaders and exert influence in government and on the street.

The third of the militia groups emerged in the security vacuum that resulted from regime change. These militias vary in size, organization, and degree of discipline. At the most local level they can consist of little more than a few thugs with guns who take control of neighborhood streets and pry support and money from people in areas they control in return for the limited protection they can offer. At the other end of the scale is Muqtada al-Sadr's Mahdi army, whose 10,000 fighters make it the largest and most cohesive. Capitalizing on a large charitable network built by his late father before regime change, Sadr has used radical anti-American rhetoric to rally disaffected Iraqis to his organization. Sadr's popularity has increased as the intervention has failed to deliver significant improvements to people's lives. The events of April and August 2004 showed that Sadr is able to launch rebellions in the south. Today, he maintains the ability to foster unrest in the key towns of Basra, Amara, Kut, Nassiriya, Najaf, Kufa, Karbala, and Baghdad. Ominously, the geographic spread of these uprisings indicates that smaller militias and armed gangs have used Sadr's confrontation to assert their own autonomy against the fragile Iraqi state. The decentralized nature of Sadr's militia continues to cause problems. In spite of Sadr's repeated calls for calm in the aftermath of the al-Askari shrine bombing in February 2006, units associated with the Mahdi army have been blamed for most of the violence in and around Baghdad.

The murderous disorder unleashed last February left many in Baghdad and Washington wondering who controls the militias. The majority of militias were created in the aftermath of regime change or imported into the country in 2003 and have since expanded their numbers rapidly. Their political leaders have had trouble maintaining control over them. Even Sadr's own Mahdi army, considered to be one of the more centrally organized militias, with full-time fighters being managed by local offices and receiving between $250 and $300 a week in pay, is showing signs of strain. Groups within the Mahdi army are reported to have rebelled against Sadr's control or refused to obey specific orders. With so much money being made by militias involved in kidnapping and extortion, their local financial, if not political, independence is growing. Sadr's recent sermons in Kufa have focused on the severe penalties that will be faced by those within his organization who flout his authority, a further sign that fissures have begun to appear.

Although most of the indigenous militias took shape in response to the security vacuum, they strive to justify their assertions of control by embracing sectarian ideologies and posing as guardians of their respective ethnic or religious communities. Across Iraq, but particularly in the south of the country, militias have targeted local police departments, infiltrating their members and placing their own senior commanders in regional management positions. In May 2005 this led the police chief of Basra, General Hassab al-Sade, to declare that he had lost control of three-quarters of his force. The gravity of the situation was highlighted in September 2005, when two British undercover soldiers were seized by members of the Basra police force. (The British army was forced to rescue them from a police barracks when intelligence suggested that a militia faction within the police [the Jamaet] was planning to move them to another location.)

The conduct of the police and their management in the south of the country has not been a problem just for coalition forces. The Ministry of Interior in Baghdad has also become the focus of a series of scandals. In November 2005 the U.S. military raided a detention facility run by the Ministry of Interior in a Baghdad suburb. Inside they found 170 illegally held detainees, a number of whom were malnourished and had been tortured. Of greater concern were the actions of the special commando forces directly recruited, trained, and managed by the Interior Ministry. John Pace, upon his retirement as director of human rights for the United Nations Assistance Mission in Iraq (UNAMI), accused the ministry in February 2006 of "acting as a rogue elephant within the government." The focus of his attention was the ministry's counterinsurgency special commando units, who have been repeatedly blamed for sectarian killings in Sunni areas of Baghdad. In addition, evidence has been accumulating of collusion between the ministry's commando units and the militias themselves, with uniforms, weapons, and vehicles being lent to the militias to help them operate more effectively. Even the new minister of Interior, Jawad al-Bolani, who is reputedly independent of any one party or militia, was forced to travel to Najaf to meet Muqtada al-Sadr at the end of October 2006 to gain his blessing for policies aimed at reforming the ministry.

INTERNAL VERSUS EXTERNAL CAUSES OF INSTABILITY

The illusion that an American victory can be retrieved is sustained by a misdiagnosis of Iraq's tragedy. The administration and its supporters see al-Qaeda and Iran working to undermine an essentially responsible, moderate indigenous Iraqi center. If the tempestuous violence instigated by Iran and al-Qaeda were forcefully countered by U.S. and Iraqi troops—their reasoning runs— a viable centrist coalition would be free to form. The president's announcement of new, presumably wider rules of engagement for U.S. forces in Baghdad flowed from this assessment. Conversely, failure to stand up to Iran and al-Qaeda would grant them strategic success and signify the retrenchment of American power. Senator Joseph I. Lieberman (I-CT), for example, argues that Iran is a "sponsor" of the Mahdi army, the militia loyal to Muqtada al-Sadr—an unlikely situation, given Sadr's nationalist leanings and his rivalry with Iran's SCIRI client. Although Iran has apparently provided elements of the Mahdi army with money, weapons, and improvised explosive device (IED) know-how, the latter possibly through Lebanese Hezbollah, there is little evidence that the Mahdi army is a creature of Iran, or that the Mahdi army relies exclusively or even largely on Iranian support, or that it would wither if Iran were to withdraw the assistance it now provides. The Iraq NIE concurs in this view, judging the violence in Iraq to be self-sustaining, albeit accelerated by attacks carried out in the name of al-Qaeda and the Jaish al-Mahdi.

Furthermore, the "external factor" explanation overestimates Iran's interest in stoking such terrible violence just across its border with Iraq. For Tehran, a weak but peaceful neighbor ruled by a Shia government best meets its strategic needs. Iran is deliberately cultivating a degree of economic dependency in Iraq by supplying electricity, cooking gas, cash subventions, and financial credit to Shia markets. (Iran is setting up at least three banks in Iraq.) Iran is also thought to be establishing a clandestine military structure for the purpose of attacking U.S. forces in the event of a confrontation over Tehran's nuclear program. Bleeding the United States, of course, serves multiple objectives: It embarrasses an adversary, probes its weaknesses, and hastens its departure. On the other hand, chaos in Iraq does not serve Iran's political, economic, or military objectives particularly well. This is true of Syria as well, which also has the blowback of radical Islamic activism to fear.

The emphasis on al-Qaeda as a decisive factor in Iraq's disorder fails to account for the radicalization of the broader indigenous Sunni opposition and the increasingly blurry lines between al-Qaeda in Iraq and other segments of the Sunni insurgency. That there are Iraqis who espouse the jihadism of al-Qaeda is beyond doubt, just as there are hundreds of foreign fighters in Iraq. As suggested earlier, the use of Islamist language and symbols has grown across the board. But the extent to which this signifies an umbilical link to an external al-Qaeda that can manipulate Iraqi politics is open to doubt.

The more supportable view is that turmoil in Iraq is due largely to internal factors. The annihilation of civil society by a succession of disasters—Ba'athist rule, sanctions, and invasion—has closed off the near to medium term possibility of normal, national politics. Outsiders, whether American, Iranian, or Syrian, are not in a position to shape the evolution of Iraqi politics in a conclusive way. Iraqis have distinctive visions of Iraq and their places in it. That they are prepared to manipulate third parties to advance their respective agendas is only natural. But this does not imply effective foreign influence. Thus, Prime Minister Maliki rejects benchmarks, demands the removal of U.S. military roadblocks from Sadr City, and forbids the arrest of an al-Sadr deputy; Abd al-Aziz al-Hakim shelters Iranian intelligence officials at his compound shortly after being hosted by President Bush at the White House; Muqtada al-Sadr berates "Persians" after visiting Tehran and declaring that the Mahdi army will help defend Iran against American attack; and some Sunni insurgents say they are prepared to talk to the United States while still others refuse to talk to the occupier or its "puppet government."

Influential policymakers and experts argue that irrespective of whether Iraq's root problems are external or internal, a robust and sustained U.S. military commitment to Iraq is inextricably linked to the broader credibility of the United States as a security guarantor. From this standpoint, reputation is the cornerstone of deterrence, and disengagement from Iraq before it is stabilized would inevitably invite new challenges to U.S. interests. The historical record, however, suggests that credibility is not necessarily cumulative. In reality, rivals constantly reevaluate one another's capabilities in the overall context of the prevailing strategic environment. They do not, typically, hurl dramatic challenges toward their competitors on the basis of what their rival did or did not do in the past and under different circumstances. Admittedly, this is truer of states than of terrorist organizations of Hamas's or al-Qaeda's ilk, which tend to project episodes from their respective enemies' past onto the present in a rigidly simplistic way.

Whether the United States stays or goes, global jihadis and their supporters will believe that they have already won twice over: first, by virtue of the intervention, which confirmed their narrative, and second, by creating the appearance of having thwarted Washington's allegedly imperial designs. A U.S. decision to disengage militarily from Iraq will reaffirm these beliefs. However, given the size of the propaganda victory the United States has already conferred on Islamic extremists, and the way that U.S. military operations continue to confirm the jihadi worldview, a decision to remain in Iraq so as to avoid emboldening radicals is inevitably quixotic. As to the administration's concern that disengagement would weaken the resolve of regional states to counter the jihadi threat, the fact is that chaos in Iraq has been used by Sunni governments in the region to justify their resistance to reform and to legitimize repression. A loss of will, therefore, is scarcely the problem. The more pressing issue is the effect of backpedaling on reform on the growth of radicalism.

Even if rival states, such as Syria and Iran, or global jihadis, are momentarily emboldened by a managed American disengagement, the central question is whether that cost would outweigh the blow to American credibility of floundering ineffectually in Iraq while supplying the Muslim world with iconic images of seeming weakness and cruelty. If a viable Iraqi political center is unachievable in the meaningful future, the answer must be no.

The complicating, painful consideration is that of moral obligation. An ill-informed and ill-prepared Anglo-American intervention, launched primarily to serve U.S. security objectives, unleashed the horrors of the past four years. Consequently, the United States incurred the duty to leave Iraqis no worse off than on the day of the invasion, and, if possible, better off. The bleak truth remains that the United States is incapable of restoring Iraq even to the relative stability of the Ba'athist era, let alone the comparatively Edenic condition of Egypt or Jordan. The even bleaker truth is that continued U.S. military operations on Iraqi territory might well leave Iraqis even worse off. In that light, for the U.S. government to sacrifice the lives of its soldiers in the pursuit of an unattainable objective (a stable, pluralistic Iraq aligned with U.S. interests) or an inappropriate one (reputation for toughness and reliability) would be the least morally defensible course that Washington could take. That is not to say that the U.S. obligation to Iraq is somehow nullified; incapacity stemming from the absence of will or competence cannot excuse a moral agent from ethical obligation. But the will and competence are simply unavailable.

In retrospect, George F. Kennan was correct when he told the Senate Foreign Relations Committee in 1966 that, "[T]here is more respect to be won in the opinion of this world by a resolute and courageous liquidation of unsound positions than by the most stubborn pursuit of extravagant and unpromising objectives."

THE CASE FOR DISENGAGEMENT

THE CASE FOR STAYING: THE ADMINISTRATION'S NEW WAY FORWARD IN IRAQ

On January 10, 2007, the president disclosed his plan to augment the U.S. force posture in Iraq with 21,500 troops to be deployed in the coming months. (Although the troop surge received the most attention, the plan also includes political, economic, and regional elements.) The purpose of this surge is to restore order in Baghdad. According to Stephen J. Hadley, national security adviser to the president, without the surge, "The Iraqi government and its security institutions could fracture under the pressure of widespread sectarian violence. Chaos would then spread throughout the country—and throughout the region. The al-Qaeda movement would be strengthened … Iran would be emboldened and could be expected to provide more lethal aid for extremist groups. The Kurdish north would be isolated, inviting separation and regional interference. Terrorists could gain pockets of sanctuary throughout Iraq from which to threaten our allies in the region and our security here at home." These developments could well follow a U.S. disengagement, which President Bush argues would force U.S. troops to fight "an uglier battle" elsewhere. In view of these stakes, as Vice President Richard B. Cheney has made clear, the surge is going to take place regardless of public or congressional opposition. Thus, the issue is what happens after the surge. Since General Petraeus has said that he expects the results of the surge to become apparent quickly, the "day after" realities should be thought through now.

FALSE HOPES

Although conditions for the success of a surge strategy are poor because of the already fractious state of Iraq politics, the disproportionately small number of U.S. troops allocated to the effort, and the relatively short projected duration of the effort, a positive result cannot simply be ruled out; there is necessarily a glimmer of hope, however fleeting. Hope has also been placed in other proposals, some of which would complement a surge effort and others that would differ in focus.

None of these alternatives would be likely to yield acceptable results. The salient proposals include:

- **Rejiggering the coalition.** Taking steps to strengthen the government, as Hadley proposed in a December 2005 internal memorandum on Iraq, is unlikely to turn things around. Washington is scarcely capable of effective measures "to help [Maliki] form a new political base among moderate politicians from Sunni, Shia, Kurdish, and other communities." Exhortation, as in the president's January 2007 address to the nation, is also unlikely to work.

- **Taking sides.** The alternative, choosing sides, poses its own problems. Sunnis and Shia already regard the United States as an ally of their respective enemies. The Shia resent American demands for power sharing, while Sunnis are aggrieved by Washington's installation of the Shia as the country's rulers. These perceptions have gained traction despite strenuous, if unsuccessful, efforts by Ambassador Zalmay Khalilzad to project an evenhanded American stance. A change in posture would have substantial regional implications. If the United States were to side with the Shia—the so-called Eighty Percent Solution—its relations with traditional allies in the Persian Gulf and Middle East would be jeopardized. To side with Sunnis would be to back the apparent loser within Iraq and possibly to spur Iranian intervention; it would certainly embolden the Sunni "dead-enders" the United States has been trying unsuccessfully to subdue or lure into negotiations. (It would, however, be consistent with an evolving U.S. policy designed to solidify a regional Sunni bloc.) As much as taking sides is not in Washington's interest, it is essential to acknowledge that cooperation with and support for the current Iraqi government is tantamount to taking sides. The issue is therefore unavoidable. Even disengagement will not extricate the United States from this bind, especially if the Iraqi government requests continued military aid, including arms transfers. Nevertheless, overt alignment with either party would transform a failed attempt to implant democracy into a seeming attempt to subvert it, further compromising America's reputation in the region and beyond.

- **Reaching for stability via devolution.** Separation of Iraq into a loose federation or clutch of ministates is another chimera. The country is already being divided, either because the government in Baghdad has disenfranchised largely Sunni regions or because cleansing operations in some mixed areas in and around Baghdad—projected to be a multiethnic city under one of these plans—and other cities are proceeding unimpeded by either the Shia government or the United States. Fully one-third to one-half of Iraq's local minority populations is already displaced, either within the country or on the other side of its borders with Syria and Jordan. The Kurdish zone, in any case, is already largely autonomous. As envisaged by Leslie H. Gelb, president emeritus of the Council on Foreign Relations, and Senator Joseph R. Biden Jr. (D-DE), there are attractive, sensible elements to federalization, including sharing of oil revenues and increased reconstruction assistance, both of which are already centerpieces of the administration's program. Peter W. Galbraith's somewhat more radical approach to decentralization also foresees an equitable division of oil revenue. The Iraqi government, if not precisely moving in the opposite direction, is certainly not rushing to pass a hydrocarbon law and does not seem likely to fulfill its promise to revise the constitution in a way that guarantees a share of oil revenues to the Sunni minority.

It is as an operational matter, however, that devolution would be most problematic. The sectarian populations to be segregated would have to consent to the arrangement. Many would object. In the case of the Sunni population, particularly in the south, the resistance has shown its determination to prevent displacement. Fighting between Sunnis and Kurds trying to eject them from Kirkuk, a vital Kurdish objective, would seriously complicate U.S. efforts to carry out a separate plan. Resistance to population transfers elsewhere could turn violent. Given that over half of Iraq's population is concentrated in four mixed cities, the safe separation of populations under either the federalization or decentralization scenarios would require additional American troops; international police would not suffice. The forces necessary for this mission are not available.

- **Concentrating on training Iraqi forces.** Leaving behind U.S. training personnel or advisers who could not defend themselves would be imprudent, especially since they would not make a decisive difference in the loyalty, reliability, and effectiveness of the Iraqi forces to which they were attached. Very few units would benefit from this kind of assistance now. Any U.S. advisers who were embedded in Iraqi units would be at far greater risk of assassination or abduction than their comrades in training units. The deployment of special operations advisers would be appropriate only in exceptional cases in which the U.S. command and Iraqi governments identified superior potential for vital missions, such as suppressing death squads or insurgent cells, renditions, defending the Green Zone and vital installations, or protecting reconstruction teams.

- **Withdrawing from the cities to the borders.** Pulling troops back to Iraq's long, porous borders to keep infiltrators out, control refugee flows, or, in the north, to discourage Turkish intervention would have little political or military value. As long as U.S. forces are on Iraqi soil in large numbers, the United States will be stigmatized as an occupier. In fact, redeployment within Iraq might simply reinforce fears that the United States seeks a permanent presence in Iraq despite the administration's disclaimers. In any case, there are not enough Americans in Iraq to seal the borders.[2] Basing U.S. forces in the Kurdish area would also run counter to Washington's interest in a unitary Iraq. Moreover, while basing of U.S. troops might function as a deterrent to Turkish intervention, by the same token it could eventually encourage the sort of provocative Kurdish behavior that will ultimately provoke the Turks. On balance, the Kurds are somewhat more likely to exercise caution without the United States providing what would in effect be a trip-wire deterrent to Turkish intervention.

- **The "Halfway House" Approach.** The search for a way to limit U.S. military exposure, reduce casualties, preserve regional credibility, and sustain fading U.S. domestic support for the war while still accomplishing worthwhile goals has spurred the suggestion that only half the U.S. troops in Iraq be withdrawn. The remainder would be redeployed to western Iraq to fight the Sunni insurgency and to cities where minority communities are in danger and need to be resettled under American

---

[2] The number of troops needed to patrol Iraq's borders, using the number of U.S. Customs and Border Protection and National Guard personnel on the U.S.-Mexico border as a guide, would be at least 20,000—not including the logistics, support, and headquarters assets that they would need. Even though the agents and soldiers on the U.S.-Mexico border know the terrain well and many have a command of Spanish, they apprehend only about one-third of those who get across the 3,141-km. U.S.-Mexico border; in comparison, Iraq's border stretches 4,071 km. It would take almost the entire planned troop surge—20,000 of the 21,500 soldiers—to *begin* to secure Iraq's borders. And even then, the level of security would be no better than that at the Mexico border. (Calculations are based on data provided by the *CIA World Factbook*.)

protection. This concept is not unlike the twelve-to-eighteen-month disengagement plan advocated by this report, in which the decreasing but still large U.S. military formations in Iraq during the disengagement period would be redeployed to suppress al-Qaeda and other Sunni insurgents and to protect and, if necessary, move vulnerable sectarian minority communities to safe locations. The difference is that under the various "Halfway House" concepts in circulation, the large residual force would remain in Iraq indefinitely, despite the diminishing returns and increasing cost of their continued presence.

HOW TO DISENGAGE

The presence of American troops cannot prevent an internecine conflict that is already raging. Whether the violence meets the textbook definition of a civil war, in which two armed groups square off to control the territory of a state, is immaterial. Iraqis are killing one another systematically and in large numbers; according to the UN, more than 14,000 have lost their lives since June 2006 alone. If there are more than two contending factions, that means only that there are multiple, simultaneous civil wars. Accordingly, the United States should withdraw the bulk of its military forces from Iraq within twelve to eighteen months and without reference to Iraqi progress toward national reconciliation. That said, the administration owes it to the Iraqis, who have suffered immensely, and to Americans, who have invested precious lives yet face a now more dangerous world, to put more thought and planning into the exit from Iraq than it invested in the entry.

In practical terms, that means carrying out the disengagement in coordination with the Iraqi government and, as necessary, armed groups outside of it and that U.S. forces in the queue for redeployment are put to good use. A further step would be to convene a group of UN Security Council members, Japan and Canada, and states bordering Iraq, including Syria and Iran, to participate in a regional stabilization project. Its purpose would be to encourage Iraq's neighbors to pursue their common interest in a unified, stable Iraq in mutually reinforcing ways.

The intention to withdraw should be declared as the results of the surge become clear. A coordinated declaration of this kind would not entail setting a certain date on which the last

American soldier would depart Iraq. Since there exists a remote possibility that the situation on the ground might change radically during the drawdown period, the United States could qualify its declared intention to leave on a specific timetable with appropriate caveats. If, for example, there were a dramatic increase in intercommunal violence leading to a flood of refugees, U.S. forces might be needed to set up camps, administer aid, and provide security for the refugees. Alternatively, if the current surge strategy works, political compromises are made, ethnic cleansing operations cease, militias are brought under the government's control, a multiconfessional army including a meaningful number of Sunni officers is created, and the United States is asked to remain to battle a lingering insurgency, it might behoove Washington to suspend the drawdown. A twelve-to-eighteen-month time frame for disengagement, to commence once the results of the surge have become apparent, would leave the United States with the flexibility to respond to such changes. The surge results should be clear well within six months. Nevertheless, the departure timetable would not hinge on specific benchmarks, since the Iraqi government is probably incapable of curbing militias and accommodating Sunni concerns; nor is it likely to generate an effective, multiconfessional army in the foreseeable future. The U.S. drawdown should not be hostage to Iraqi performance.

U.S. military disengagement would not mark the end of America's involvement in Iraq. Withdrawing the bulk of our military forces from the country will however change the nature of America's commitment to the Iraqi people. The U.S. embassy would continue to administer large-scale economic, commercial, and technical assistance, maintain robust intelligence liaison and collection efforts, as well as a defense cooperation program.

To provide a quick reaction capability to the U.S. command and signal to regional states that disengagement from Iraq does not signify abandonment of the region, a robust combined arms force should be deployed on the periphery of Iraq. There are several basing options: For large units, which would be required if there were an imminent threat of the Green Zone being overrun or a humanitarian catastrophe, Kuwait would have the capacity and motivation to provide access; for "drive-by" interventions necessitated by the establishment of al-Qaeda camps in western Iraq, the detection of networks working from specific urban locations, small, specialized units based in eastern Jordan and out of the public eye would be feasible and not impose an undue political burden on Jordan's King Abdullah II. The diplomatic and legal framework for these deployments is largely in place, but the United States should nevertheless open negotiations with basing countries as it coordinates the drawdown of U.S. forces with the Iraqi government. A dual-track approach will help offset doubts about Washington's commitment to the region that are bound to arise as the United States removes its forces from Iraq.

Troops or technical experts and equipment would be deployed to installations outside of Iraq to monitor cross-border movements for intelligence collection, interdiction, or preparation for humanitarian operations. Training of selected Iraqi units could continue on a small scale at installations outside of Iraq, much as police training has been conducted in Jordan, although admittedly without great success so far. Advisory personnel might be attached to selected Iraqi units whose reliability is assured. A robust force would remain in the Green Zone and Baghdad International Airport (BIAP) to protect access routes and deter a direct assault on the U.S. embassy in the event that order breaks down.

During the disengagement period, the United States should focus on combating the Sunni insurgency, patrolling Iraq's borders, and training especially promising Iraqi units, much as commanders on the ground in Iraq have been doing in the absence of guidance from Washington, but without serious expectation of either stanching the insurgency or producing highly competent Iraqi formations. The unfortunate fact is that the few competent units stood up during this interval will run into logistical and financial difficulties later on as U.S. technical support to the Ministry of Defense is reduced upon disengagement of U.S. forces.

Overall, disengagement can be expected to diminish deterrence in the short term; it will surely be blamed for any increased violence. The U.S. response to these criticisms should emphasize the sacrifices the United States has already made, continue American efforts to stabilize Iraq diplomatically and economically, and manage the humanitarian dimensions of the civil war, especially refugee flows.

The United States' priority at this stage should be to limit the effects of the civil war and, at worst, confine it to Iraq itself. This enterprise should include a multilateral effort to alleviate the humanitarian hardships that Iraqis are enduring. The current conflict caused a dramatic increase in refugee flows that began in 1991. This is not just a potentially destabilizing burden for moderate states like Jordan. Past experience has shown that large concentrations of refugees incubate irredentist violence and nourish jihadism. Coping with these flows will require the coordinated efforts of the UN, wealthy donor countries, and nongovernmental organizations

(NGOs). There is a major role here for U.S. forces and technical assistance, either or both of which could be provided to countries that face burgeoning refugee problems.

U.S. military disengagement from Iraq will not occur in a vacuum. Countries in the region may attempt to influence the timing and nature of America's disengagement from Iraq to suit their own national interests. This dynamic process must be managed through an intensive program of diplomatic coordination, including Iran and Syria. The administration is understandably reluctant to confer tacit recognition on unsavory regimes that believe, with some reason, they have the whip hand. The fact remains that their cooperation in a stabilization plan for Iraq is indispensable. Syria, according to the U.S. command in Iraq, is permitting about sixty foreign jihadis per month to enter Iraq. Although the Iraqi insurgency is largely indigenous, jihadis may have been used to carry out some of the devastating suicide attacks that have spurred Shia reprisals. A combination of pressure and inducement might persuade Damascus to constrict if not cut off this supply of potential suicide bombers. Iran has supplied Shia militias with weapons and funding and, by virtue of its proximity, the size of its intelligence presence, and cross-border Shia networks, Tehran could probably nudge Iraqi Shia toward accommodating some Sunni political requirements while getting the militias to cut back on their anti-Sunni activities.

Syria and Iran might regard a conciliatory U.S. approach not as an appeal to mutual interest but rather as a source of increased leverage to put forward their own demands as to, respectively, Syria's interests and activities in Lebanon and the December 2006 UN Security Council sanctions resolution against Iran. Tehran might want concessions in the nuclear arena while Damascus would probably seek some accommodation to its goals in Lebanon, assurances that the investigation into the murder of Lebanon's Prime Minister Rafik Hariri will not touch core regime members, and renewed attention to the Golan Heights problem. Although a U.S. offer to facilitate Syrian-Israeli talks would be feasible, concessions in other areas would be incommensurate with Syria's actual ability to help Washington on Iraq. Concessions to Iran in the nuclear domain would be too high a price for Tehran's help, given that a stable Iraq is in its interest and Iran's capacity to affect Iraqi politics in a decisive way is uncertain at best. The stakes, however, demand that the possibility of cooperation be actively explored and that reservations about talking to Iran and Syria be subordinated to America's paramount interest in a stable Iraq. With respect to Iran, a multilateral framework might relieve the administration of the need to drop suspension of enrichment activity as a precondition for bilateral discussions. There is room for doubt on this score, however. Since the Iranians themselves have not yet linked cooperation on Iraq to the nuclear issue, for Washington to insist on linkage even as it consented to work with Iran in a multilateral forum might still be counterproductive. Washington would have to feel its way on this question, deciding after the Iranians had reacted to the initial proposal for multilateral talks. This overall approach could also entail direct U.S. talks with the Iraqi nationalist section of the insurgency. Discussions have already taken place on a desultory basis, but a U.S. decision to withdraw might alter the dynamic for the better.

There is no guarantee that Syria, Iran, or members of the insurgency would engage in such a venture, or do so on terms acceptable to Washington. A multilateral framework, in which the U.S. presence would be diluted and other countries can bring their influence to bear, might make it easier to persuade Syria and Iran that their interest in a stable Iraq is best separated from other policy priorities. Hence, the importance of creative multilateral diplomacy. Multilateral talks would also help mobilize Gulf Cooperation Council (GCC) funds essential to put Iraqis to work and provide an honorable alternative to service in the militias; enlist the Saudis to persuade Sunni nationalists to disavow and suppress the jihadis among them rather than complicate the situation by dispatching Saudi militants, funds, and weapons to Iraqi Sunnis, and to respond positively to conciliatory Shia gestures that might eventually surface; allay Turkish concerns about developments in the Kurdish areas; and help Jordan cope with a tidal wave of refugees. For the greatest possible leverage on regional players, especially regarding the need to block the transfer of weapons to the contending parties within Iraq, the diplomatic process should weave in Chinese, Russian, and European Union (EU) participation.

An explicit U.S. commitment to pull out the bulk of American troops from Iraq on a timetable to be negotiated with the Iraqi government might prove useful in persuading the relevant parties to cooperate in a stabilization arrangement. Iraqi leaders and all the major Arab parties, both Sunni and Shia, in the government of national unity have publicly called for U.S. troops to leave as soon as possible. At the same time, the nationalist insurgents—so called to differentiate them from the jihadi component of the insurgency—have insisted that their precondition for negotiating with the Iraqi government or the United States is a timetable for the disengagement of American troops. If presented by the U.S. administration with such a timetable, most members of the Iraqi cabinet, parliament, or wider political elite would not voice opposition but instead use their leverage to secure continued financial and logistical assistance from the United States. While the insurgents might merely wait out the U.S. military pullout and then intensify their challenge to the government, there is a roughly equal probability that they will perceive an increase in their bargaining power and at least experiment with negotiation. By sponsoring talks, the UN would lend weight to the diplomatic process and increase incentives to participate. A UN monitoring and implementation group could also help stabilize the disengagement process.

Neither the fact of the war nor its intensity will likely abate upon the disengagement of U.S. forces because Iraq's Sunnis will continue to fear the ultimate consequences of the reversal of fortune that they perceive the Shia as seeking to complete. The real question is how much worse the bloodshed can get. A credible—although many might say optimistic—forecast is that the lack of organizational capacity, broad communal consent, and heavy weapons on either side militates against a drastic increase in the already appalling casualty rate. Crucially, the largely Sunni areas are of little interest to the Shia as objects of desire or conquest. And without artillery, armor, and attack aircraft, Shia forces will be far less capable of reducing Sunni majority cities, such as Falluja, to rubble, in the way that Serbs dealt with Croatian or Muslim urban areas in the former Yugoslavia. Ethnic cleansing in mixed areas will continue to advance, the large flow of refugees and internally displaced will continue to mount, massive bombings and death squads will continue to claim many lives, but crucial conditions for nationwide genocidal violence are as yet absent. This probabilistic judgment is hardly a cause for rejoicing: It only suggests that a bloody stalemate between similarly equipped adversaries is somewhat more likely than the annihilation or expulsion of Iraq's Sunni population. Nevertheless, the consequences of such escalation are so extreme that the United States should begin working now with the UN, NATO, coalition members, and neighboring states on plans for a rapid multilateral intervention in the event that genocidal warfare breaks out after the withdrawal of U.S. forces.

A related question is whether the disengagement of U.S. forces in the near term would open the door to a regional war triggered by the civil wars within Iraq. As noted above, direct armed clashes between or among the armies of Iraq's neighbors do not seem to be in the cards. Although history is not always an infallible guide, mid-to-late- twentieth-century civil wars in the region—in Algeria, Yemen, Afghanistan, Pakistan, and Lebanon—have not sparked bigger wars. In most cases, surrounding countries have tried to protect their interests through proxies while avoiding the risks and costs of military intervention. Even Lebanon, whose civil war ultimately drew in both Syrian and Israeli forces, did not mushroom into a true regional war. Damascus and Jerusalem both took steps to prevent escalation. Indirect conflict, however, is probably inevitable, especially in the absence of a diplomatic process designed to stave off or at least regulate moves by neighboring countries to protect their interests using proxies. Indeed, this low-profile competition is already under way. To the limited extent that the presence of U.S. military forces can stave off a regional war stemming from the violence in Iraq, such a presence could and should be kept in-theater. But it should not be in Iraq.

Finally, there is the issue of al-Qaeda's presence in Iraq. Clearly, al-Qaeda has succeeded in establishing a strong presence in western Iraq. How durable it proves to be and how focused it will be on attacking Americans remains to be seen. Opinions on these questions differ within the intelligence community. Nevertheless, the spread of the jihadi ethos within the insurgency does not bode well. Nor does the development of urban warfare skills among the jihadis, including the effective use of snipers and IEDs. These techniques could be used in European cities, for example, as well as in Ramadi. Jihadis have been urged by Ayman al-Zawahiri to attack targets outside of Iraq. Abu Musab al-Zarqawi, the late leader of al-Qaeda in Iraq, masterminded an attack in Amman that claimed many civilian lives. The presence of large numbers of Iraqi refugees in Jordan provides useful cover for jihadis looking to operate in that country. Moreover, the so-called ratlines that bring foreign fighters into Iraq can support the reverse flow of terrorists to other regional cities or onward to western Europe.

The jihadis' ruthlessness gives than an edge for now in their quest to dominate the insurgency. For example, they recently killed four leading tribal Sheikhs and, in effect, compelled others to seek refuge in Jordan and Syria. (Al-Qaeda in Afghanistan has applied the same tactic to the tribal *maliks* in the Federally Administered Tribal Areas along the Pakistan-Afghanistan border.) Against a background of increasing convergence between the supposed nationalist insurgents and the religiously oriented jihadis, this momentum could conceivably lead to an al-Qaeda ministate in western Iraq. If this were to happen, the United States would be confronted with an urbanized, cellular version of al-Qaeda's rural presence in Afghanistan prior to 2002.

The question is, will the departure of U.S. forces foster these developments? It looks as though foreign fighters go to Iraq both to kill Americans and because it's easier to attack enemies of Islam in Iraq than elsewhere. (One Lebanese fighter told an interviewer that it was easier to enter Iraq than to penetrate the Israeli border and attack the near enemy.) It seems more than likely that in the absence of U.S. troops in Iraq, the flow of outsiders will dwindle over time. While it is true that the cross-border movement of refugees complicates the work of Jordanian and Syrian security forces, these states muster the resources to stay on top of al-Qaeda infiltration. The United States works closely with the Jordanians and, on a halting basis, with Syria. The latter relationship has been impeded because of tensions raised by other issues. As suggested earlier, these impediments could be put aside in the interests of both sides in tamping down al-Qaeda activity.

Upon the departure of U.S. forces, the more mainstream elements of the insurgency seem likely to turn against the smaller jihadi groups whose ferocity has thus far given them a disproportionately large role. There is a precedent for this process in Algeria during the mid-to-late 1990s, when local village militias—in effect, death squads—were raised to challenge the Armed Islamic Group (GIA). The creation of the Anbar Salvation Council, an Iraqi tribal group funded largely by the United States, might well develop in the way that Algerian anti-jihadi groups did a decade ago. At the same time, the Salafi element within the insurgency will focus more intensely on its Shia enemy within Iraq. This trajectory is not guaranteed, however, and there remains a serious chance that an al-Qaeda-linked, Salafist organization might dominate the Sunni provinces for an indefinite period.

Thus, the cities of western Iraq might still become safe havens for al-Qaeda operatives who steer clear of confrontations with other insurgents and take advantage of the relative safety of their neighborhoods, the availability of transit routes in and out of Iraq, and the abundance of materiel to stage attacks outside of Iraq. This raises the question of whether the continued long-term presence of five U.S. combat brigades, the current planning estimate, is the best way to counter the threat. If the deployment of troops to Anbar, a fiercely nationalistic region, is indeed a spur to violence, the continued presence of U.S. forces is likely to be counterproductive. Instead, the United States should continue to work closely with groups like the Anbar Salvation Council and to build up local Sunni police organizations that can gather and act on intelligence regarding Sunni extremists. This is essentially an intelligence and law enforcement task. The availability of highly mobile, specialized U.S. forces at bases in Jordan can support the operations of indigenous units once the bulk of U.S. combat forces have been withdrawn from

Iraq. Until then, the United States could profitably use the interval to help recruit, organize, train, and support local units for the counterterrorism mission.

WHY NOT WITHDRAW NOW?

If the situation in Iraq is so dire, its prospects so bleak, the use of force futile, and the daily toll so grim, why put military disengagement on a twelve-to-eighteen-month timetable? Why not draw down U.S. forces immediately? In the first instance, an immediate disengagement is probably not possible without leaving much if not all of the heavy equipment behind—vehicles, armor, artillery—because bulky materiel cannot easily be moved by air, the only way to exit swiftly. Transporting the large amount of materiel in Iraq by sea would take months in part because of transit times and in part because of limits on the availability of the appropriate cargo vessels and port capacity. In addition, a safe and orderly disengagement hinges on carefully planned, choreographed troop movements that cannot be executed in haste. Logistical and tactical factors alone militate against the instantaneous redeployment of the 160,000 troops that will be in Iraq once the surge is complete.

There are also compelling strategic reasons to draw down in a deliberate fashion. In disengaging, the United States must seek to shape the narrative of its intervention in Iraq in order to preserve the greatest possible credibility in a painfully compromising situation. Thus, the United States would want to avoid the appearance of a rout or panicky departure. Nothing, for example, must be left behind that is not expressly intended for use by the Iraqi government or future use by U.S. forces or other personnel. Troops destined for other bases in-theater will need the way paved diplomatically and in military-to-military channels with their new host countries. This process will take time. A hasty, apparently ill-organized or poorly coordinated departure will shake the confidence of friends and embolden adversaries at the worst possible time. On the ground in Iraq, the drawdown will have to be done in a way that deters attacks by insurgents. At root, shaping the narrative comes down to ensuring that no American leaves under fire from the embassy roof in a helicopter. It also means that as many as possible of Iraqi nationals whose security is at risk because of their cooperation with the United States are given safe passage to the United States. A methodical disengagement will necessarily be carried out at the cost of additional American lives, a bitter but unavoidable price.

Finally, a twelve-to-eighteen-month disengagement time frame dictated by logistical, tactical, and "narrative shaping" factors has the additional virtue of providing a large if steadily diminishing U.S. troop presence in Iraq for a limited but crucial period, during which the Iraqi government has pledged to pursue a national reconciliation agenda and rein in the militias. Thus, within the first part of this time frame, a determined Iraqi government will not find itself militarily abandoned by Washington.

RECOMMENDATIONS

The steps prescribed in this report should be initiated immediately, before the costs of the war begin to widen. They are already in the air: a looming threat to Jordan's stability; the empowerment of a radicalized Iran; rise of ominous anxieties in Turkey and the Persian Gulf states; strained alliance relations; Washington's prolonged distraction from seething problems in Afghanistan, Pakistan, and Palestine; the weakening of Arab moderate voices; fuming animosity toward the United States throughout the Muslim world; reinvigorated jihadi sentiment; and of course the direct cost measured in the loss of American blood and treasure. Each year of continued U.S. military operations in Iraq will consign over 1,000 American soldiers to their deaths and three times that number to crippling injury. The economic costs of the war are also massive, even for an economy as large as that of the United States. The direct cost is $8 billion per month, though how much is actually being spent in Iraq per se is unclear since the Iraq war, as a budgetary category, is subsumed under the line item for the Global War on Terrorism. The total cost for the wars in Iraq and Afghanistan in 2007 is now projected to approach $170 billion. The administration disclosed in early February that it will ask Congress for a $145 billion supplemental appropriation for FY 2008. Depending on the way in which the surge unfolds, this figure might increase, as will casualties generated by the application of more permissive rules of engagement in dense urban settings.

Another potent reason to move forward sooner rather than later lies in the possibility of things going wrong in ways that Washington has failed to foresee, or which are by their nature unforeseeable. In the first category: The Sunni insurgents get better at battling U.S. and Iraqi forces; the Shia militias both expand and continue to fracture while improving their own combat capabilities; the United States suffers the equivalent of the 1982 Beirut barracks attack or loses an aircraft to an insurgent surface-to-air missile; British forces are caught in a confrontation that causes severe losses, leading to their disengagement; a sectarian leader—Sistani or Sadr—is assassinated; Shia affiliated with the Iraqi government are implicated in a particularly horrendous atrocity against Sunnis; a U.S. unit duplicates the Haditha massacre on a larger scale; U.S. military recruiting and retention goes into free fall; or the United States and Iran come to blows because of a confrontation on the ground between Iranian personnel and U.S. forces attempting to take them into custody or as the result of U.S. strikes against Iran's nuclear-related infrastructure. These are just examples of things that could conceivably complicate the U.S. position. The mishaps that actually occur will be different and probably more vexing.

As it prepares to withdraw militarily from Iraq, the United States should act decisively and creatively across the wider Middle East to offset perceptions of American weakness that our setback in Iraq has triggered. The obvious arena for action is the triangle formed by Israel, Lebanon, and the Palestinian Authority. Iran and its Syrian ally believe themselves to be ascendant. With the United States having eliminated Iran's adversaries to the east and west and then gotten bogged down in an Iraqi civil war, Tehran's bravado is perhaps understandable. Yet its challenge must be met. Withdrawing from Iraq might enable the United States to use its resources, leverage, and residual credibility to counter the influence these countries bring to bear on Lebanese and Palestinian politics. Less plausibly, but still conceivably, it might also improve prospects for a more assertive international response to Iran's apparent pursuit of a nuclear weapons capability. At a minimum, military disengagement will remove one of many obstacles to effective action. This is not meant to suggest that the disengagement of U.S. military forces from Iraq will somehow usher in a new golden age for the United States or the countries of the region. Full recovery from its misadventure in Iraq is likely to take the United States many years.

Indeed, the project to rebuild American credibility will face two stark limits. First, no possibilities will open up for the United States in the region until it has successfully managed its disengagement from Iraq—a necessary though not sufficient condition for rebuilding U.S. influence. Second, the weakness of the protagonists on both sides of the Palestinian-Israeli divide is likely to hobble any return to negotiations, although an Israeli-Syrian return to negotiations might be a productive alternative. Similarly, the challenge posed by Iran's nuclear ambitions will not easily be met. It is beyond the scope of this report to devise a diplomatic strategy to deal with the complex and hugely difficult problems entailed by the Lebanon-Israel-Palestine impasse or the dispute over Iran's nuclear enrichment program. They are all the more difficult because Americans are palpably demoralized by the miscarriage of their huge effort in Iraq. Yet there is no reason to doubt the American capacity to overcome this calamitous episode and work with partners toward a safer and better future in the greater Middle East.

The United States should:

Declare its intention to disengage the majority of U.S. combat forces from Iraq within twelve to eighteen months, to begin once the results of the surge become known.

- Retain the forces necessary to secure Baghdad International Airport, the Green Zone, and access routes that connect them.
- During the disengagement period, stage the drawdown to maintain the forces in Iraq needed to protect or relocate vulnerable minority populations and suppress insurgent activity in the largely Sunni provinces.

Shift focus to containment of the conflict and strengthen the U.S. military position elsewhere in the region.

- Plan for humanitarian contingency operations.
- Refocus on containment of the war in Iraq.
- Reinforce the U.S. military presence elsewhere in the Persian Gulf region, for example, Kuwait; explore options for increasing special operations forces deployed to Jordan; and increase the number of rotational deployments to the region, including joint exercises.

Engage Iraq's neighbors, including Iran and Syria, members of the UN Security Council, and potential donors in a stabilization plan for Iraq.

- Prepare to provide Jordan with help in managing the cross-border refugee flow.
- Work with the UN secretary-general to form an Iraq stabilization group, including Iran and Syria, with an emphasis on control of borders, management of refugees, economic and technical assistance to Iraq, and diplomatic support for political reconciliation.
- Work with the UN, NATO, and neighboring states on plans for humanitarian intervention in the event that violence in Iraq becomes genocidal.
- Act decisively elsewhere in the region, particularly on the Palestine-Israel impasse by articulating a vision for final status, and on support for Lebanese sovereignty.

ADVISORY COMMITTEE MEMBERS

R. Rand Beers
NATIONAL SECURITY NETWORK

Stephen Biddle
COUNCIL ON FOREIGN RELATIONS

Anthony H. Cordesman
CENTER FOR STRATEGIC &
INTERNATIONAL STUDIES

Christine H. Fox
CENTER FOR NAVAL ANALYSES

F. Gregory Gause III
UNIVERSITY OF VERMONT

Ellen Laipson
HENRY L. STIMSON CENTER

Steven E. Miller
JOHN F. KENNEDY SCHOOL OF
GOVERNMENT

William L. Nash
COUNCIL ON FOREIGN RELATIONS

Thomas R. Pickering
HILLS & COMPANY

Barry R. Posen
MASSACHUSETTS INSTITUTE OF
TECHNOLOGY

Eric Paul Schwartz
CONNECT US

Walter B. Slocombe
CAPLIN & DRYSDALE, CHARTERED

Note: This report reflects the judgments and recommendations of the author(s). It does not necessarily represent the views of members of the advisory committee, whose involvement in no way should be interpreted as an endorsement of the report by either themselves or the organizations with which they are affiliated.

ABOUT THE AUTHOR

Steven N. Simon is the Hasib J. Sabbagh senior fellow for Middle Eastern Studies at the Council on Foreign Relations. Prior to joining the Council, Simon specialized in Middle Eastern affairs at the RAND Corporation and was the deputy director of the International Institute for Strategic Studies in London. From 1994 until 1999, Simon served as director for global issues and senior director for transnational threats on the National Security Council staff. He has published widely in leading foreign policy journals and newspapers and is a frequent commentator on radio and television. He has a BA from Columbia University in Classics and Near Eastern languages, an MTS from the Harvard Divinity School, and an MPA from Princeton University. In addition to teaching at Georgetown University, he has been a university fellow at Brown University and Oxford University. Simon is the coauthor of *The Age of Sacred Terror*, *The Next Attack*, *Building a Successful Palestinian State*, *The Arc: A Formal Structure for a Palestinian State*, and coeditor of *Iraq at the Crossroads: State and Society in the Shadow of Regime Change* with Toby Dodge.

RECENT COUNCIL SPECIAL REPORTS
SPONSORED BY THE COUNCIL ON FOREIGN RELATIONS

Darfur and Beyond: What is Needed to Prevent Mass Atrocities
Lee Feinstein; CSR No. 22, January 2007

Avoiding Conflict in the Horn of Africa: U.S. Policy Toward Ethiopia and Eritrea
Terrence Lyons; CSR No. 21, December 2006

Living with Hugo: U.S. Policy Toward Hugo Chávez's Venezuela
Richard Lapper; CSR No. 20, November 2006

Reforming U.S. Patent Policy: Getting the Incentives Right
Keith E. Maskus; CSR No. 19, November 2006

Foreign Investment and National Security: Getting the Balance Right
Alan P. Larson, David M. Marchick; CSR No. 18, July 2006

Challenges for a Postelection Mexico: Issues for U.S. Policy
Pamela K. Starr; CSR No. 17, June 2006 (web-only release) and November 2006

U.S.-India Nuclear Cooperation: A Strategy for Moving Forward
Michael A. Levi and Charles D. Ferguson; CSR No. 16, June 2006

Generating Momentum for a New Era in U.S.-Turkey Relations
Steven A. Cook and Elizabeth Sherwood-Randall; CSR No. 15, June 2006

Peace in Papua: Widening a Window of Opportunity
Blair A. King; CSR No. 14, March 2006

Neglected Defense: Mobilizing the Private Sector to Support Homeland Security
Stephen E. Flynn and Daniel B. Prieto; CSR No. 13, March 2006

Afghanistan's Uncertain Transition From Turmoil to Normalcy
Barnett R. Rubin; CSR No. 12, March 2006

Preventing Catastrophic Nuclear Terrorism
Charles D. Ferguson; CSR No. 11, March 2006

Getting Serious About the Twin Deficits
Menzie D. Chinn; CSR No. 10, September 2005

Both Sides of the Aisle: A Call for Bipartisan Foreign Policy
Nancy E. Roman; CSR No. 9, September 2005

Forgotten Intervention? What the United States Needs to Do in the Western Balkans
Amelia Branczik and William L. Nash; CSR No. 8, June 2005

To purchase a printed copy, call the Brookings Institution Press: 800-537-5487.
Note: Council Special Reports are available to download from the Council's website, CFR.org.
For more information, contact publications@cfr.org.